June 25, 2001

So, here I am lying in my bed. I just bought this journal today, along with an ASP 3.0 book. Not really an eventful day... I worked 8½ hours at Lockheed, came home, ate smothered burritos that Leah made and took it easy the rest of the evening. I just got off the phone with Kristen. We had a great conversation about all the many things that are going on in our lives right now. I am working nearly 60 hours a week @ two jobs. And Kristen is in Ft. Collins studying hard at Staff Training. Tomorrow is probably the biggest day of our relationship thus far. We find out whether Kristen is going to be placed in the regional office in California or in Austin. All our hopes and dreams lie in Austin. Neither of us really have any desire to live in CA. But somehow God has really given me peace about the whole situation. Not the kind of peace that says we will definitely be in Austin. But the kind of peace that tells me that God is in complete control. It's only by giving our lives completely over to God that we can find true freedom. It sounds like an oxi-moron, but when you think about it in the spiritual rhealm, it all makes sense. Somehow I know that God will keep and protect Kristen and I no matter where we are. Does that mean that things don't get tough sometimes? Of course not. So as I get ready to fall asleep I can only give God the praise for giving us the change to serve in ministry. I pray that no matter the outcome tomorrow, We can still give our lives completely to Christ and rely on His strength all the days of our lives.

Well, I don't think I'm going to write a lot tonight. I'm tired and need to wake up around 5:30 for work. So... today, today. What went on today? Work was long. I only worked 8 hours and I was incredibly drained. I'm working on a login script that will run off of SQL Server 7. What a pain. So I was exhausted on the way home and Kristen called and complained about me not taking initiative and coming up to see her. I wasn't that I didn't want to see her, it was just that I was trying to get Saturday night off work so I could come up and surprise her. She was hoping that I would come up so we could celebrate her placement in Austin. Yes, we found out last night that we are NOT going to CA! Praise God! Anyway, Kristen and I ended up talking about the

the situation and I was able to
explain to her that it frustrates
me when I can't plan to surprise her
or even think about making a proactive
effort to see her because she
can be so impatient. She finally
realized where she was wrong
and apologized to me. What an amazing
woman. I am truly blessed to have
Kristen in my life.
So, then Biff, Kate, and I went
and played tennis. We stopped by
Krispy Kreme on the way home
and here I am now. Long day.
Oh, and I have this big ugly zit
on my forehead! I am really
ready for the skin to clear up. Anyway
TMI. That's all... nighty night.

August 11, 2001
1:57 pm

Well, I know it's really been a long
time, since I've written. It's not
that I haven't wanted to, it's just
that it seems like it's hard to find
any free-time anymore. It feels like
all I ever do anymore is work.
I worked tonight, at Piatti, and
Monday I start my last official
week of my internship. Overall things
are going pretty well.
   Today is Kristen and I's 4 year
anniversary. Time has really flown by.
They say that time flies when you're
having fun, and the last 12 months
has been nothing but.
   Spiritually I think I'm doing
pretty good. Sometimes I feel like
I'm barely hanging in there, but
I'm thankful that God has given
me a lot of determination. I truly
believe that I am a perfectionist
in many ways. I mean, there

are times when I couldn't really care less about something, and yet other times when I really push myself to do something right. I suppose this is why I really get hard on myself at times. I know that God can, will, and does forgive me when I sin. But sometimes the hardest thing for me to do is forgive myself. I wish I could learn how to show grace to myself and others. If I had one prayer for my spiritual walk right now it would be for that one issue. I pray that God would sustain the fire within me for His son and that I wouldn't have to guess whether or not I've sinned or strayed from His side.

Well, I'm ready for bed and very very sleepy. Sorry for the delay! Talk again soon!

Well, here I am... lying in bed
about to fall asleep. I know it's been
a long time since I've written, but
I've decided that I really want to
be persistent in writing so that I
can remember more about my
past and hopefully grow from it as
well.

Today I had to put together a
demo notebook with some of the
art I've done for websites. I
went to Kinko's, well I thought
I went to Kinko's, but exiting
@ beltline only got me 9/10 of the
way there. The damn Car Toys parking
lot blocked the way to Kinkos and
the frontage road was one-way.
Anyway... I spent $10 to get some
color prints + computer time and
then headed home. At 2:30 I
had an interview/meeting with the

communications director at church.
They need someone to do logo's and
other image work for the church.
The position only pays 25k, but
it's ministry, so I guess I sort
of expect it. That job looks like I
might have a 50/50 chance, but
Carlyle - the communications director said
that "East West Ministries" may need
a webmaster. So that sounds like
an even better fit for me. After
that I, headed over to Kristens and
we went and got an oil change in
her car. Then we went to Vernonia-Abba
and logged my 27 hrs of work on
their website. For dinner, Kristen, her Dad,
kyle and I all went to Compisi's for
pizza. Kathryn is in mexico at a
"FAT FARM". Then after this Kristen
went out with Alexis & Alyssa and
I went home with the guys and
watched the opening ceremonies for

the 2002 Salt Lake Winter Olympics. Overall nothing really eventful happened. My walk with Christ is going well right now, but the trouble finding a job has tested my trust at times. Anyway, Kristen should be calling anytime to say goodnight so I will now say goodnight. Goodnight!

Tues. Feb 12, 2002

Well, I'm lying here in bed thinking about my evening. Tonight Kristen came over and I made spaghetti. After dinner Kristen sat and worked on save the date cards for atleast an hour. All the while Chris, Brian, and I were watching the Olympics. Kristen and I then decided to go sit in the hot tub - very romantic. Thursday is Valentines day and I ordered a dozen roses to be delivered to Kristen. For a guy without a job they were very expensive. $80 on the VISA. But it's worth it. Just to see her smile would be worth all the money in the world. Anyway... so we came back from the hot tub and Kristen left about an hour later. Kristen is so funny. When she was leaving I walked her out to her car and a simple kiss turned into a very funny moment. I was joking around and blew into her mouth while kissing. She decided to do it back and practically spit all over me. It was really funny. Also, before I sign off... tonight was the first time Kristen farted in front of Chris. Believe me... it was not one of those "moments to remember". Kristen is so special.

I am truly a blessed man.

Published by te Neues Publishing Company
16 West 22nd Street, New York, NY 10010
Tel: (800) 352-0305, Fax: (212) 627-9511
and te Neues Verlag, Am Selder 37, D-47906 Kempen, Germany
Tel: (02152) 916-0, Fax: (02152) 916-111
www.teneues.com